1 PAGE ONLINE MARKETING GAMEPLAN

Get More Leads and Make More Money Using Social Media and Online

Sam Mahmud

10-10-10
Publishing

1 Page Online Marketing Gameplan
www.onepagegameplan.com
Copyright © 2021 Sam Mahmud

ISBN: 979-8504477-39-8

References to internet websites (URLs) were accurate at the time of writing. Authors and the publishers are not responsible for URLs that may have expired or changed since the manuscript was prepared.

Limits of Liability and Disclaimer of Warranty
The author and publisher shall not be liable for your misuse of the enclosed material. This book is strictly for informational and educational purposes only.

Warning – Disclaimer
The purpose of this book is to educate and entertain. The author and/or publisher does not guarantee that anyone following these techniques, suggestions, tips, ideas, or strategies will become successful. The author and/or publisher shall have neither liability nor responsibility to anyone with respect to any loss or damage caused, or alleged to be caused, directly or indirectly by the information contained in this book.

Publisher
10-10-10 Publishing
Markham, ON
Canada

Printed in Canada and the United States of America

Contents

Foreword

I heard of Sam Mahmud before I met him, and was referred to him as a marketing genius. He is very passionate when he talks, and is a gentleman at heart. When you meet Sam, you will find nothing extraordinary about him, apart from his infectious smile. He is always smiling.

Social media is perhaps the most dominant platform for marketing. The ability to hyper-target an audience gives you an immeasurable advantage. If you are an entrepreneur, running a small business, or trying to grow your business, then Online Marketing Gameplan is a solid point of reference. The strategies and methods discussed here are well tested.

Sam is also an accomplished coach and speaker. His solid background, stemming from his work in the financial sector, gives him an edge which is uncommon and well cherished. This is someone who walks the talk.

In uncertain times, your adaptability will give you stability. Insights like this make this book a compelling handbook for marketing yourself digitally. Sam has distilled the essence of using social media as a potion for marketing success.

Raymond Aaron
New York Times Bestselling Author

Acknowledgements

I would like to thank my mom and dad for raising me to be the person I am today and showing me the value of hard work. I would not have been able to achieve all my success if not for the endless love, admiration, guidance and patience from my parents. Mom and Dad, you are the best.

I am extremely grateful to one of the most amazing persons in the world, Juhaina Binth Junaid, my partner in crime and life. There is a reason why you are the better half.

I would like to acknowledge Kevin Green, founder of Wealth Management. I am a member of the Wealth Management Group, and it's been a transformational experience for me. Kevin has encouraged me to take risks, learn new things and move on from my nine to five job. I admire his extensive knowledge on everything from properties to how to manage wealth, and I have been greatly inspired by him.

I am part of a business networking group called BNI. BNI consists of chapters based in local regions, and the chapter I belong to is called BNI Rendezvous. I would like to thank the following members from my power team: Amit Patel, Dillan Gandhi, Nishit Kotak, Rishi Bhuptani, Virr Haria, Anita Amoa, Danny Eastman, Debesh Das Gupta, Rizwan Mohammadali and Sanjay Gohil. Special mention to Tom Leigh at BNI Bentley for being an amazing partner. Thank you for inspiring me every day. And thank you, Rishi Bhuptani, for getting me into BNI.

It takes a network to write a book. I am thankful to Raymond Aaron and his team for making this happen for me. This book wouldn't have been possible without Raymond's insight, knowledge and guidance. The great thing about working with Raymond was his candid insight into being objective and subjective in the matter of getting the book done.

I am thankful to Roger Hamilton. I attended one of your seminars, and it has changed my views on how I want to grow as an entrepreneur. What struck me as amazing was your depth of knowledge about how to grow companies.

I deeply appreciate the wisdom of Phil Berg. His insights have helped me to view sales as an attitude, and to find opportunities to create that difference in my life. Phil talks with amazing passion that inspires you to the core.

I need to mention Ben Fisher. Ben is a like-minded digital marketing guru who's always double on the cutting edge. He's always got some amazing insights on digital marketing trends, and I am always learning from him.

To the staff and Secretary General of Commonwealth Secretariat. Commonwealth Secretariat is an amazing international institution based in London, and it was my first workplace. Working there taught me to be humble, to appreciate diversity and to recognise talent.

Jamie Dimon is the CEO of JP Morgan, and I've had the amazing fortune to work in his organisation. Jamie, I have probably read your biography 10 times, and you have been an inspiration. I shook your hand once and would love to do so again.

I would like to thank the rest of my chapter in BNI. This is a group of remarkable people, and I am so lucky to have each and every one of them sharing this amazing journey. I am eternally grateful to my chapter for supporting me and my ideas. These are the members who have kept me humble and focused over the years: Amit Patel, Anita Amoa, Bhaven Ondhia, Bhavni Shah, Bunmi Oguntunde, Conan Sammon, Danny Eastman, David Margo, Debesh Dasgupta, Dillan Gandhi, Francis Okeke, Howard Brown, Howard Sherbourne, James Lai, John Grant, Justine Davies, Kevin Tyson, Nilesh Patel, Nishit Kotak, Paul Mcdonald, Raji Ashwin, Rishi Bhuptani, Rizwan Mohamedali, Sanjay Gohil, Sheila Chadha, Shreena Kothari, Sue Rick, Sukumal Wimaladarma, Vinny Parmar, Virr Haria and Yewande Adigun.

*"When I hear people debate the ROI of social media?
It makes me remember why so many businesses fail.
Most businesses are not playing the marathon. They're
playing the sprint. They're not worried about lifetime value
and retention. They're worried about short-term goals."*
Gary Vaynerchuk

Chapter 1

What Is Your Business Objective?

A t the end of the day, success in your business will depend on 4 different things:

1. Your business idea: how creative your business idea is.
2. People who surround you: can also be your access to the talent pool.
3. Sales: how quickly you can grow your client base.
4. Customer Service: how long you can retain your client base.

The power of social media when harnessed properly will perhaps become your cheapest source of getting your client base in order.

Strategy Versus Tactics

Tactics is organic. It's something that happens on a day-to-day basis, whereas a strategy needs to be discussed and deliberated. Thinking of how you can compete against your competitors is exactly how you should be setting your strategy.

Your strategy should define competitive advantage, how you allocate your resources, your long-term vision and objective and your brand positioning. It is important to keep the strategy simple if you are a start-up or a small business. As your business grows, your strategy will become more mature and more complex over time, and it's better not to overcook it from the get-go. It is vital to have a solid strategy because this is how businesses become successful, and it differentiates you from your competitors.

Take Action Now

Fill out the "What is your goal?" section of the **My 1 Page Online Marketing Gameplan** sheet.

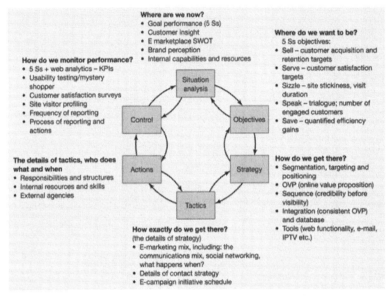

Source: https://www.smartinsights.com/

Strategy Shows Long-Term Vision

You need to have specific targets for specifically reviewing performance. Without this, it will be just adding noise to your overall processes. It doesn't need to be a hard number; it can be a softer version, but it is important so that you know how to communicate

4

your directions, since these are the communications to your employees and stakeholders. A solid strategy should have a well-defined vision, goals, objectives and a guideline to resource allocation.

Brand Positioning

Once your avatar is defined, which is basically a definition of the audience, a strategy should define how your brand should be perceived by your audience.

Resource Allocation

As it becomes important to allocate your resources properly, the strategy should have specific budget, time, people and any other resources correctly allocated.

Source: https://www.slideshare.net/

"Strategy without tactics is the slowest route to victory.
without strategy is the noise before defeat."
Sun Tzu (~500 BC)

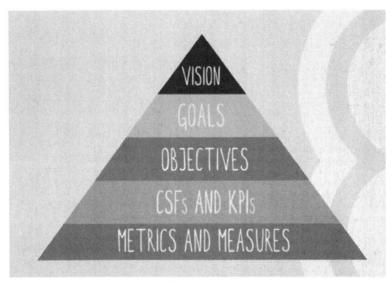

Source: https://www.smartinsights.com/

What Is Your Business Pitch?

When you are selling online, it's important to know how to pitch your products/services. If you're in a face-to-face meeting, you can have other members of your team there during your pitch. This shows that everyone involved in the decision-making process is in the room, and it shows the seriousness of the account.

Your objectives must be measurable and quantifiable. In my client meetings, I always ask my clients how they would define success. Success can be getting yourself something that ends up with a number: It can be a number of followers; it can be an amount of sales;

it can be a number of leads. Unless you have the measures in place, you would most likely be investing your money without any real impact.

Bring members of your team to the meeting so that the client knows who they will be working with, and be sure to introduce your team members to the client.

Do a profile on the target market for the advertising campaign, and present your research by describing the target audience and their product preference. You should show how the product factors into the advertising messages. Show how your messages differ from that of the competitor.

Is Social Media Cheap?
Is It Cheaper to Advertise on Social Media?

Social media advertising is not cheap. A lot of business owners often misinterpret the concept of putting content online. You can always open an account on social media for free, but when it comes to marketing, more often than not, I find that the business owners are wrong.

More often than not, I often find that the business owners hire and trust a single person in the whole organisation to manage all of their companies' social media channel. A successful social media marketing campaign needs continuous effort and support from a team .The team supports researching the market, collecting the data, and finding influencers that fit your business, content and the actual execution of the campaign.

My 1 Page Online Marketing Gameplan

	What Is your goal?	Are you selling products or services? Define your target market.	What channels should you use to reach your target market?
Prospecting			
	How are you capturing leads?	How are you keeping your leads warm?	How are you converting your leads?
Maturing Leads			
	First-class business in a first-class way	Upselling and repeat selling	Make the longer-term campaigns cost-effective.
Customer Retention			

Notes

Notes

Chapter 2

Define Your Target Market. Are You Selling a Service or Are You Selling a Product?

Selling a product is very different from selling a service online. The underlying objective and difference here is that a product is a tangible object, whereas service is value added through time, intangible skills and expertise.

The costs and techniques vary between products and services as well. Here are some thought processes to help you understand and appreciate the right approach for your business.

Product-based selling: Products are designed to meet the needs of the customer. So when you're selling a product, you would want to highlight the features/attributes and display the items appropriately online or in-store. With products, it's easier for customers to appreciate the value. In the unlikely circumstance that they don't like a product, they can simply return it. They can also leave a review online for prospective customers; and in turn, the prospective customers can make a decision on the back of the reviews as well.

Whether you choose to run a product business or a service business, it is important to do your research and understand how best to satisfy your customers.

Service-based selling: These businesses are usually less expensive to operate than product businesses because you don't have to maintain an inventory. And it typically requires building a relationship with the customers when necessary.

Getting the pricing right for a service is often time consuming. This will vary between industries, as well as the experience of those operating in these industries. It is also more difficult to get ratings because it takes longer to get a service completed or for it to take effect.

Whether running a product-based business or a service-based business, you need to take note of what your competitors are doing, what your prospective clients are looking for and how you can meet the demand. Once you start getting the customers, you need to control and continually evolve the process, and make necessary changes to the process. This is where you continually evolve your selling strategy.

Take Action Now

Fill out the "Are you selling Product or Services? Define Your Target Market" section of the **My 1 Page Online Marketing Gameplan** sheet.

The biggest risk is not taking any risk...
In a world that is changing really quickly,
the only strategy that is guaranteed to fail is not taking risks.
Mark Zuckerberg

Notes

Notes

Chapter 3

Which Social Media Channel Is Right for Your Business?

3

In uncertain times, your adaptability will give you stability. Adaptability in times of uncertainty also creates opportunity. Your business should be adaptable to embrace any social media channel that will get you leads and conversions.

Each social media channel plays a different role in users' lives. There are also particular social media channels that are banned in certain countries or regions. So, when selecting the best social media channel for your business, you should always look at:

- What engagement you're getting.
- Which audiences use that particular channel.
- What kind of campaign you're running (service or product).
- Your budget.
- How long you are going to run the campaign.

Facebook and Instagram are great for getting client engagements, whereas LinkedIn will get you a lot of organic leads. LinkedIn is more suitable for professional networks, whereas Facebook and Instagram are more suited to personal level networking. However, Facebook is unavailable in China, so if you're targeting your Chinese customer base, you are probably better off using WeChat. TikTok is gaining a lot of ground recently, but again, it lacks engagement beyond a certain age range.

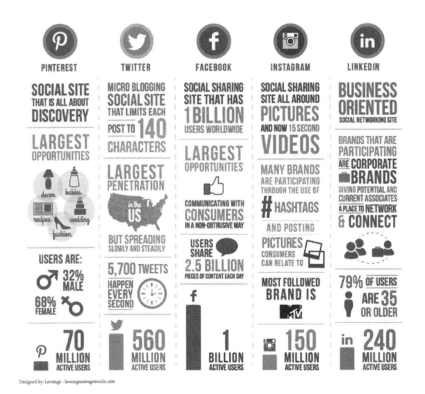

What Should Be My Budget?

Most companies spend about 5% to 20% of annual revenue on marketing. Between 35% and 50% of this should be allocated to digital marketing activities; and depending on the social media sector you are in, spend can be anything up to 50%. Basically, your overall marketing strategy should play a role in how much money you want to spend on social media. You also have to be cautious to not cannibalise your marketing budget from FCO, content marketing, display advertising and other trending marketing activities.

Take Action Now

Fill out the "What Channels Should I Use to Reach My Target Market?" section of the **My 1 Page Online Marketing Gameplan** sheet.

Digital marketing investments (next 12 mo.)

Q: What are your company's plans for investing in the following digital marketing areas over the next 12 months?

N = 244 marketing managers   RANKED BY PLAN TO INCREASE

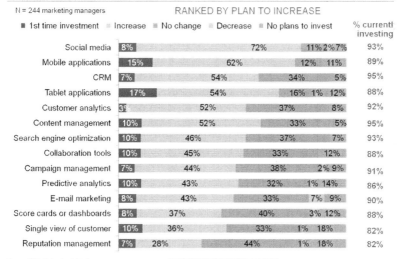

	1st time investment	Increase	No change	Decrease	No plans to invest	% currently investing
Social media	8%	72%	11%	2%	7%	93%
Mobile applications	15%	62%	12%		11%	89%
CRM	7%	54%	34%		5%	95%
Tablet applications	17%	54%	16%	1%	12%	88%
Customer analytics	3%	52%	37%		8%	92%
Content management	10%	52%	33%		5%	95%
Search engine optimization	10%	46%	37%		7%	93%
Collaboration tools	10%	45%	33%		12%	88%
Campaign management	7%	44%	38%	2%	9%	91%
Predictive analytics	10%	43%	32%	1%	14%	86%
E-mail marketing	8%	43%	33%	7%	9%	90%
Score cards or dashboards	8%	37%	40%	3%	12%	88%
Single view of customer	10%	36%	33%	1%	18%	82%
Reputation management	7%	28%	44%	1%	18%	82%

GARTNER FOR MARKETING LEADERS

Notes

Notes

Notes

Chapter 4

How to Catch the Leads

S ocial media is awesome for building awareness, getting the right traffic and getting the right leads.

Know which keywords are trending.

Social media gives a certain amount of transparency in terms of what interests lie out there. It's important for a marketer to understand the trend and keep an ear out in terms of the conversation between a brand and a customer.

- Keep an eye out for the conversations unfolding on social media. This includes keeping an ear out on the channels such as YouTube, Instagram, Facebook, LinkedIn and Reddit.
- Once you have a firm grasp, you might want to join in the conversation. This will probably not translate into a sale straight away. However, this is a great approach to get into the hearts and minds of your clients.
- You're not set up on an electronic mechanism to monitor what is being discussed about your brand and the products. I don't like to spend much time on the electronic side of things as this should be used to figure out the trending topics rather than be used as a solution as a whole.

Get the Right Message Across

The quality of the content will determine the engagement you receive. You don't need to be overly sales minded in your content to generate more leads. Establish yourself as an authority or an expert who has the right resources and the helpful information. Once the credibility is established, you are likely to get more leads.

https://www.engagebay.com/

Getting the right message is very important. There needs to be a right balance between the postings, and as mentioned earlier, it is important to be objective about conversations and sales. Also, each social media channel contributes and reacts differently. LinkedIn is great for professional updates, whereas Twitter is great for immediate responses. Facebook is great for engagements, whereas YouTube is great for video explanations. With all these social media channels, the emphasis should always be on sharing the content, which in turn contributes to the traffic and, eventually, leads.

Funnels, Funnels, Funnels

Converting leads into customers takes a bit more work than what meets the eye. To convert a lead into a paying client, some rules of thumb might be useful here:

- Your social media page should exactly translate your offerings.
- A purchase event should never be more than three clicks away.
- All landing pages and product offerings should be easy to understand.
- Make appropriate use of images and videos. Use images for infographics, and videos for explanations.

Take Action Now

Fill out the "How Are You Capturing Leads?" section of the **My 1 Page Online Marketing Gameplan** sheet.

An Offer Too Hard to Resist

Often, you'll find yourself asking, "How can I make my products and services more compelling? Why are people not buying my products or services?"

Sometimes a product is not selling, simply because the offer is not correct. Having a good product is important of course, but a good product by itself may not sell. You have to package it with an irresistible offer.

Get the correct title of your product. So instead of calling your product "Subway," you want to call it "Subway sandwich" or "Subway footlong sandwich." See, the more descriptive you are, the better you are communicating the product to its audience.

The pricing of the product needs to be in competition with other products in similar offerings. Your product needs to stand out from its competition; and to make it irresistible, you have to show the reason why you are asking for that price.

Discounting a product works well, and it's been time tested over and over again. You take advantage of an important day or an important event, and it will get people through the door. Once they're in, they might buy non-discounted products from your shop as well. So this one is a no-brainer.

Giving out a bonus, especially a free bonus, works pretty well too. So say when someone is subscribing to your service (for argument's sake, a beauty product), you could give them an autographed copy of the beauty product. Even if you can't think of a relevant product, it's still worthwhile offering something rather than nothing.

Bundling several products together and selling it at a discount, which may be a virtual discount or no discount at all, is a neat idea. As long as you're offering more than one product or service, this is a great way to get customer loyalty. Cable companies do this all the time; they offer telephone, television and internet services as a bundle, and this keeps the client for longer.

You can always take the risk out of a purchase by showing elements of a free trial or a money-back guarantee. You are essentially taking the risk out of a purchase, and clients love this because they can always return a product or service if they simply don't like it.

The offer is only valid for 14 days. What does this mean? It means that you're adding urgency to an offer, and it's an offer that people may want to make use of right now. This is a very powerful tool, and it shows the scarcity to get your product moving. Amazon uses this technique by saying, "Only X amount of stock left."

Notes

Notes

Chapter 5

How Are You Keeping Your Leads Warm?

Social media is a great way to keep your leads warm. Get them to follow you on platforms like Facebook, Instagram, Twitter, LinkedIn and YouTube. This will ensure they see your newsfeed and the latest happenings in your business. Use pay-per-click targeted ads through social media to always keep your business in clients' minds.

Use a CRM. This is important because this is how you will be managing your leads in one place and following up on leads. Even better, some CRMs provide email functionality for you to run campaigns. This means that if you plan your campaigns correctly, and if you're pushing the right content during lean months, you can keep the leads warm without much of an effort.

Publishing the right content is so important these days. Content that is engaging and helpful as a reference goes a long way for your SEO efforts. When you're writing your content, think of adding value, and give the reader something to think about. Why? Because if the reader is finding value in your content, he will most likely share and revisit that content. This means free and organic traffic.

When you are talking to clients, it's very important that you show that you have a genuine interest in their business. Showing genuine interest will help you boost your relationship and keep your business in the forefront of their minds. You will be showing that you care, and that earns trust.

You should always work to preserve warm leads in a personalised and creative way. You need to look for any opportunity to exceed the expectations of your clients.

Run a Solid Keep-in-Touch Campaign

There are plenty of ways you can get keep in touch with your leads. The most powerful of these channels is emails, and there are many services you can use that specifically cater to email campaigns. Without regular follow-up, you risk your buyers becoming disinterested.

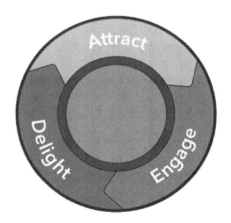

Attract Tools	Engage Tools	Delight Tools
Ads	Lead flows	Smart content
Video	Email marketing	Email marketing
Blogging	Lead management	Conversations inbox
Social media	Conversational bots	Attribution reporting
Content strategy	Marketing automation	Marketing automation

Source: https://www.smartinsights.com/

Notes

Notes

Chapter 6

How to Convert the Leads

6

Once the social media list is generated, a good marketer will take them through particular processes and nurture them into a conversion. Marketers like to call this process a sales funnel. Conversion is the final stage of turning a potential client into a paying customer. The quality of the lead usually depends on your industry campaign and objectives.

Tips on how to convert the leads:

- Offer an incentive.
- Ask for the sale.
- Simply follow up.
- Ask your lead questions.
- Show that you have a genuine interest in the person.
- Don't make the leads wait.
- Qualify the leads first.

Take Action Now

Fill out the "How Are You Converting Your Leads?" section of the **My 1 Page Online Marketing Gameplan** sheet.

Notes

Notes

Notes

Chapter 7

Keep Your Clients for Longer

7

lient retention is always paramount when you're growing your business. Frequent communication with your customers keeps you fresh in their minds and, most often than not, gives you important information. Social media is a great way to communicate with your clients on an almost daily basis.

Give your most loyal customers extra perks. This can be in the form of running competitions and giving discounts and incentives to become a loyal customer.

Provide a fantastic customer service. While this is usually a given, one survey recently showed that 51% of clients left a business because they were dissatisfied with the service. Customers remember when they are treated well or poorly, and they always tell their friends and family about their experience. So treating customers well simply means you not only get a loyal customer but also expand your client base.

Give customers a reason to be loyal, and don't forget to smile. I often run competitions during the dry months, and this achieves a couple of different objectives. A customer loyalty programme works great in this space too.

• It drives up the interest in the business.

- It shows the networking possibility within your existing network.
- It shows that you are a business that cares.
- The number of return clients picks up.

Delivering First-Class Business in a First-Class Way

In the future, there will be a lot more emphasis on creativity and quality in social media advertising. Keep a specific budget for creativity, if you aren't already.

You'll see more success in your ads if your audience finds it funny, engaging or interesting. Spending a little extra on this will mean that you can run your ad for longer, if you have the exact right ad, at the exact right time, for the exact right person.

Social media is not for everyone and, for some businesses, there are better ways to reach their clients. B-to-B companies often fall into this category. The trick, in most cases, is to separate your clients who use social media. For example, if you are using Facebook pixel on your website, you will learn a lot about the demographics and interests of users who are actively looking for your services. This might also help you get a more targeted audience for your advertising campaigns.

Take Action Now

Fill out the "First Class Business in a First Class Way" section of the **My 1 Page Online Marketing Gameplan** sheet.

Notes

Notes

Chapter 8

Upselling

Targeted traffic refers to visitors who are not just browsing for products on your site but are actively researching products before they make their purchasing decision. The conversion rates are usually higher because these users are usually leads who are about to buy and are in a mindset to buy.

Retargeting is an essential tool to build up your audience. Retargeting will place ads before those who would like to take on your service or buy the product.

You should also use upselling as their targeting mechanism because these are the clients who have already bought something from you and have confidence in the service that you are providing. Absolutely, it will also usually mean that you are trying to sell the higher value products to your targeted audience. The upselling brings a higher return on investment.

The retargeting ads serve as a reminder to people who have seen value in your products or services. As an advertiser, this will help you fine-tune your future campaigns even more.

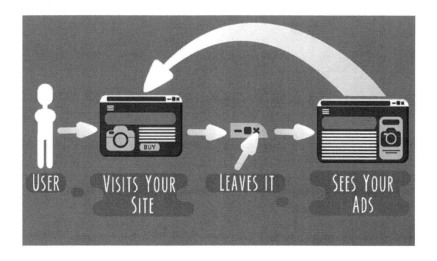

ROAS (Return on Ad Spend)

A lot of advertisers use ROAS as an acid test to measure how the ads are being run. That's how important ROAS is.

Return on investment and, in turn, return on Ad spend, is crucial. Since you can measure the ROIs easily by dividing your investment by sales, you should not be spending too much before you can evaluate and figure out how to proceed. To calculate it properly, you need to know your business goals and objectives.

The KPIs should include traffic, reach and leads, as well as comments. I have always used a bot to figure out where the interest lies in products or services before making a more substantial investment on that spend.

Once the campaign runs along for a long time and has gathered enough data to do a performance report and calculate your return on investment, there needs to be collaboration between sales and marketing specialists to track and improve the ROI.

The advantage of digital marketing is that you can continually measure and evaluate your campaigns. This will help you rework strategies and reassign your budget in the right projects.

Take Action Now

Fill out the "Make the Longer Term Campaigns Cost Effective" section of the **My 1 Page Online Marketing Gameplan** sheet.

Hyper-Targeting and the Process of Making Your Leads Cheaper

Your campaign should evolve over time. There are significant ways to hyper-target your audience and, in the process, make your ads cheaper.

Find your killer content. This is the content that will create the buzz for your brand. Don't go through a shortcut process and set your mind on something before you start your campaigns. Rather, test and test again to find out what your audiences prefer. A vanilla campaign can go through an iteration of 8 to 20 changes on creatives alone. Your content should focus on ad copy, readability and creatives.

Use your custom audience for remarketing. This in turn will give you cheaper audience targeting.

Make use of look-alike audiences. Because of the vast amount of data that social media contains on user behaviour and interests, it is much easier to find an audience that is likely to take up your services. So if the data tells you that your likely customers are in their mid-30s and living in Sacramento, you're more likely to get your money's worth by only targeting people in that age range. Social media channels, especially Facebook, are usually much more sophisticated in their audience matching. You do not even have to know what data points you're trying to match. These channels will usually do it for you.

Start your hyper-targeting with layers, by using demographics, interests and behaviour available within your target audience. For each of these categories, you can even make things a bit more granular. For an example, under demographics, you can target audiences with an upcoming birthday. Under demographics, you can even define relationships and the particular industry the individual is working in. Just imagine, from the above experience, how you can now select your audience that has an upcoming birthday, is in a relationship and is in a management position. Social media is an amazing tool when you want to target specific audiences, and if you can combine that with an attractive landing page, you'll get the best results.

You will find that the above experience doesn't fit your criteria from time to time. And it will be natural for you to combine the unique audiences together. There is usually an array of amazing diagnostic tools available, which you can use to slice and dice the targeting of your audience.

"Strategy without tactics is the slowest route to victory. Tactics without strategy is the noise before defeat."
Sun Tzu (~500 BC)

"Advertising is, of course, important because advertise is the final design. It's the last layer that speaks to the customer, that tells them what you have."
Tom Ford

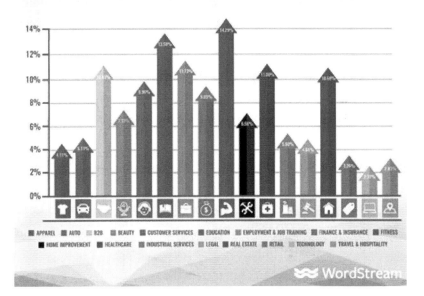

Notes

Notes

Notes

Chapter 9

What Types of Campaigns Should You Use?

Your campaign types will depend on what you're trying to achieve. Again, this is where the goals and objectives of your marketing comes into play. The types of campaigns also depend on the maturity of your organisation, and this is important because you do not want to overspend, and you also want to get the maximum bang for your buck. The type of campaign you run changes with time and technology.

Brand Promotion

1. Always add a hashtag that's recognisable to your audience. Create hashtags that make sense for your brand. You could also piggyback on current trends on social media that might relate to your brand. Piggybacking on a trend is not only free advertising; it also shows that you are in touch with the latest happenings.

2. Make sure your cover photos are top notch. This is something that should be consistent with your brand. If it's an event, it should be consistent with your event. Photos can serve as a billboard message for brands, campaigns and events.

3. In developing your YouTube channel, if videos are an important component of your social media channel on which you want to be active, then 3 to 3 1/2 minutes is an ideal length for your video. But keep in mind that engagement matters, so do as much R&D as possible to find out what exactly gets you the engagement.

4. Look after your followers. Maintain loyal followers for your brand; be quick to respond to followers in a timely manner. Well-looked-after followers will give more likes, shares and impressions.

5. Generate interest with Instagram. It's been touted that Instagram generates 15 times more engagement than Facebook. Leverage this engagement and, even better, go across channels. For example, use Twitter to link back to your Instagram page.

6. Convert your Facebook page post into an ad. An organic post on your Facebook page will only reach out to the followers following that page. When you promote that page in a Facebook ad, you will see a lot more engagement and get more bang for your buck.

7. Join the relevant public threads. It is easy to link your public posts to whatever relevant topic is ongoing. By showing that you are relating your posts to related topics only, means that you are sensitive to the world around you. This is important because it shows your brand is more attuned to the public. Sometimes it's difficult for a brand to take a stand, so rather than taking a stand, these posts should be talking about topics that are neutral to politics or strong opinions.

8. Launch new products via social media. Social media gives a variety of different creative ways to launch products.

9. Minimise negative feedback. Negative feedback is sometimes impossible to avoid, but it's a good business practise to minimise any negative feedback. There's a specific specialisation that has

evolved to manage the reputation of companies, and managing the feedback process is one of the main aims of this new branch of marketing. Always try to gather honest reviews, and always try to gather a volume of them. There are specific actions you can do to automatically send URLs that redirect to your review process.

10. Figure out the best time to make a social media update. People react to a social media update in their own time, in their own region and usually at their leisure. This also means that there will be specific time patterns as to when people are most active with their updates. Posting your social media updates at the right time simply means that you will get more engagement, which means that the social media algorithms at play will think your posting is worth sharing, and it will automatically be geared towards sharing your content more than the content of others.

11. Answer questions on social media. The questions you get are usually the queries your leads will have, which means that this is a great tool to convert any potential lead into a client. This is also a great way to expand your FAQ and make your content more comprehensive.

12. Effectively use calls to action, because you need to communicate what your offerings are. If you have a shop and you're selling something, you should say "shop now" instead of "learn more." "Learn more" implies there's more information to learn, whereas "shop now" implies that there are products offered, which means that people who are looking for that particular product will convert more easily, and this also means converting them will be cheaper.

Lead Generation Campaign

Paid ad campaigns for lead generation

Paid social media ads involve capturing vital insights and the right strategy, and using that strategy will make your media lead generation tool more effective and to the point. There are a couple of very effective tools to be used for paid ads that will help you rise above the rest.

Paid ads give you the benefit of reaching out to an exact audience, fan growth, increased engagement and much more.

Here are some tips on running a successful paid advertising strategy.

Understand your objectives

Long before you ever start spending money on social media, you really need to understand who your clients are. You need to understand the demographic you're targeting, as well as the behaviour and interests of your target audience. You would also need to understand retargeting and look-alike audiences.

Because you are now in a paid playing field, anything and everything you do is going to cost you; hence, if you know your audience well, it becomes much cheaper for you.

Creating ad funnels

This is necessary for engagement as well as testing your ads. Your funnel needs to be tested and improved over time. This does mean that you'll have multiple conversions for multiple funnels, but keep in mind that clients coming through each funnel will behave differently. For example, any client coming through funnel #1 is a longer-term client, whereas any client coming through funnel #2 needs more warming up.

Remember testing

Test, test, test. You need to test anything and everything—from look-alike clients, to interest, to behaviour, to demographics, to location—and you might even find that running ads at a specific time of day leads you to cheaper conversions.

Spend wisely

Keep an eye on the big strategy and the cost control. For example, if you bid too much, you may get great placements, but it might become unaffordable for you. The trick here is to test your ad funnel with the least amount of budget possible and then go for a bit more aggressive spending. The keyword here is to throttle rather than going for full afterburner.

Use a chatbot for lead generation. Instant messaging and chatbots are very powerful weapons for marketers if used correctly. Chat boards allow businesses to connect en masse, which also means that it will dramatically reduce the overhead cost.

Chatbots are being used by 12% of the population at any given moment. And given that the bots are omnipresent, it means that customers can reach out to you at any given moment. Chatbots can be used to extract data, do surveys, look up delivery details and much more.

Here are a couple of examples of where chatbots can be used on a regular basis:

Bots can decipher what your clients are after. So, use the bots to put in inquiries.

Bots can be used to develop and build up the profiles of clients, allowing them to deliver personalised messages, suggestions and content.

With bots, you can set up predefined messages across all social media channels.

Social marketers' top goals for social

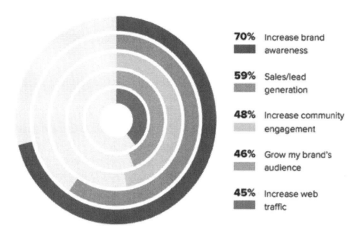

70% Increase brand awareness

59% Sales/lead generation

48% Increase community engagement

46% Grow my brand's audience

45% Increase web traffic

Source: sprout social

Bot Campaigns

We are living in the age of bots. Bots are everywhere, and if you're not making use of them, you are missing out on an important tool that's already available to you. A lot of businesses are not able to see their customers in person, and depending on their size, a lot of businesses are not able to source big teams for support, or administrative staff.

Why are bots important? Because they interact with your clientele, whether they're going to your website and calling you or finding you through social media. And these are potential leads that you want to convert. Bots are a form of automation and are a great way to get into a conversation with the client.

A big challenge for the chatbots is to process natural language processing, and a common way to avoid any unrecognised answers in the bots can be an implementation of commonly picked answers, which in turn lead a client down a decision tree. Nevertheless, the bots are becoming much more sophisticated over time, and this will potentially be a known issue in the future.

Here are 5 levels of bot marketing strategy that you can make use of:

Automatic responders:

This is the bare-bones version of automation in Facebook that's already available. Regardless of what the user says, it's basically an auto responder to say that "we have got your message and we will get back to you as soon as possible." This is a native tool, and you don't need any third party tool to achieve this.

However, keep in mind that this is a bare-bones solution, and you should only use this knowing that you will be going back to address the users' queries.

Notification strategy:

This is a very simple strategy where you are keeping your clientele aware by making a broadcast via Messenger. This is a one-way channel akin to an email, where you are simply broadcasting a message. It's useful to let your clientele know if you have a new piece of content that can be a service or a product in the offering.

There are some challenges to sending out a broadcast app notification. For example, you would have to have up to 1000 people, and delivery is not guaranteed. You can integrate third-party tools to make this happen.

Using a funnel:

This is probably the most common way to follow up on a marketing lead. It is also the most mature way to convert a lead.

Funnels can be as simple as getting the necessary information via your chat box, and taking them through several stages of warming up a client. Once they opt in via Messenger, the next step can be an email follow-up or to book a call with you, and based on the response, you can take them to a different funnel or simply convert them.

In other words, you are simply saving the contacts in your CRM, to be used in your email systems or to set up rules, work flows and similar things based on unlimited possibilities. You can even use these contacts in webinars.

Strategy deployed by artificial intelligence:

At this level, you are ready with your funnels. Your traffic is slowly building up, and you have a full strategy to grow your business and sales. You have also figured out how to handle the repetitive tasks and all the administration. Now is the time to link up your bots to an engine that understands natural language.

Dialogflow is owned by Google and is free to use. All you need to do is connect it to your Google account, and then it basically lets you create different AI agents that allow your chatbots to understand the dialogue a bit better. For example, instead of having to use keywords, Dialogflow understands the bigger picture. It basically reads the entire message, understands the context and sends a response. It is almost an interpreter to the user.

Typically, the goal for Dialogflow is to answer all user inputs. In a sense, you are building up a database of user inputs. Think of it as a child, where you are training the child to learn how to deal with an answer.

Your business and chatbots:

People who get the best results are people who understand how funnels work. And it's often necessary to understand the marketing game to be able to contribute to how it supports your business. In most cases, time is the biggest factor.

But things are always changing in this space. For example, you may optimise or change certain marketing campaigns because you have a new product or new content in the pipeline.

So when you're working with the marketing agency, or developing the strategies yourself, you need to understand how the step-by-step guideline actually works. Any marketing funnel will need regular maintenance, just like any other business process. If it's only for a very specific use—calling my phone, for example, or if it's for addressing FAQ—then it's fitting to forget about it; but otherwise, if it's a funnel, then you will likely have to keep up the maintenance.

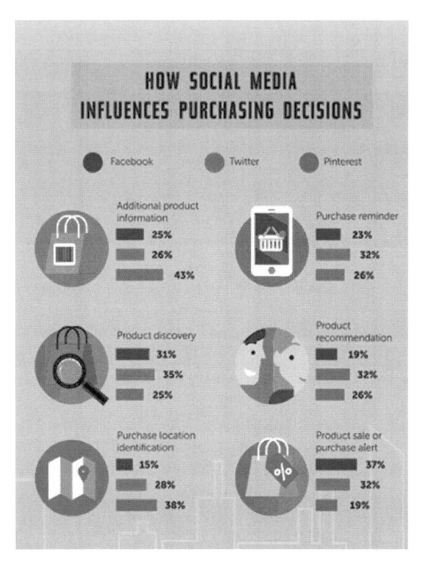

Source: https://www.business2community.com/

Conversion Campaigns

Conversion campaigns are exactly what it says on the tin. It is a campaign to convert your leads into purchases or paying subscribers. You can also use conversions to remarket to hot audiences and drive new leads or sales by targeting people who have visited your site. One thing to keep in mind as you calculate your conversion rate is the quality of the data.

Click-through campaign

This is exactly what it sounds like. A user sees your ad, clicks it and arrives on your landing page. The whole point of a click-through campaign is to get higher quality traffic to your website; and by higher quality, I mean higher paying clients, so that you can frontload more compelling content, make the content more precise and to the point, and make sure you avoid the hard sell. So here are a couple of rules of thumb that work really well with click-through, but keep in mind that these pointers are for the ad as well as the landing pages or funnels in general.

Take Action Now

Fill out the "Upselling and Repeat Selling" section of the **My 1 Page Online Marketing Gameplan** sheet.

Local Campaigns – More Foot Traffic for Your Brick and Mortar Business

Social media campaigns work pretty well with brick and mortar businesses as well. And by brick and mortar, I mean that you have physical premises and you want to increase the foot traffic.

You can do several things to drive traffic to your store, and here are a couple of ideas:

Geo location targeting:

This is also known as proximity targeting, which lets you define the area around a particular location through geo targeting. So say, for example, if your store is in a shopping mall, you can target audiences that are in the immediate vicinity, with ads showing discounts that you are offering in your store. This is a great way to increase retail foot traffic.

Offer click and collect:

Click and collect has been proven to increase sales for multiple retailers. When a customer orders a "click and collect," and then they come to the store to collect their items, it has been proven in many ways that they attempt to purchase more. Effective merchandising can increase these types of sales very easily.

Building up client relationships:

By definition, this means nurturing your clients over a longer term, rather than going for a quick sale. This makes your customer feel more valued and, over time, they will become repeat customers.

Nurturing customer communities in Facebook and LinkedIn groups is a great example of building up client relationships. Another way to build up great relationships is to ask for customer feedback.

Mind the weather:

For any brick and mortar business, weather plays a crucial role, and brick and mortar businesses should take advantage of it. For example, in summer, show ads related to cold drinks, outdoor furniture and outdoor activity; and in winter, show warm drinks and warm clothing.

Digital Media Spend Breakdown

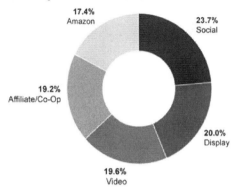

n = 283
North America/U.K. respondents with 2019 budget for digital advertising
Totals may not add to 100 due to rounding
Source: Gartner 2019-2020 CMO Spend Survey
Q. How is your company's fiscal 2019 total marketing expense budget being allocated to or spend on each of the following marketing channels? Excludes Search Advertising

Gartner.

The biggest risk is not taking any risk...
In a world that is changing really quickly, the only strategy
that is guaranteed to fail is not taking risks.
Mark Zuckerberg

Notes

Notes

Notes

Chapter 10

Why Advertising on Social Media is Cost-Effective

Most businesses are careful about their business strategies. Social media is a form of proactive marketing, and it's possibly the cheapest way you can proactively get your leads.

Your clients are using social media

This is an opportunity because at least 70% of the US population has at least one social media profile. This presents a great opportunity for businesses. Not only are your clients on social media, but they are also checking these websites regularly. Targeting these audiences is easy if you're selecting the right channels.

Consumers will take notice of your brand on social media

Social media channels are often fun to use, and they are a great way to keep in touch with friends and family. Some channels have creative implementations of games and other tools.

The reason why customers take notice of your brand on social media is because the clients can be more conversational. They can voice their opinions, or they can like or dislike a particular product or content. This is what entices them.

Increase your brand recognition

Social media has given businesses, especially the small ones, a great platform on which to be recognised across the board. Because the leads are so cheap, the small players in the market get a say when it comes to market share.

Imagine a client coming across your brand on social media. When you entice them, you will notice that they will start researching your brand.

Increase your traffic intake

Social media engagement leads to a higher amount of traffic going to your website. This basically means you get more leads, but it also means that your SEO ranking will be significantly higher.

Just think about it. Each piece of information that you put out on social media is an opportunity to bring in new leads to your website. Once the leads are in the website, it is an opportunity for you to convert, which basically means that the more quality content you publish, the more opportunities you will get for conversions.

The key to getting the most out of your social media is to strategically put your content in the channels, which is likely to convert more.

Target and retarget your clients more efficiently

The social media campaigns compliment the organic traffic very well. It's proactive marketing, and the sophistication of client targeting means that you are more likely to diversify your audience targeting, and focus on diversification as and when necessary.

With social media ads, you can define the exact interest and behaviour you are looking for in your targeting, and as you drive more traffic into your website, you keep improving the audience targeting.

Keeping it cost effective

Most of your social media interest will come from your fans and followers, and this is where investing time in good content really pays off.

Social media is usually 3X or more cost effective compared to regular media. Because of the ability to focus on particular goals and objectives in your campaign, it is relatively easy to manage your expenses and keep a lid on your budget, which in effect makes a much more sensible choice when it comes to marketing.

Improving your SEO

Search engines keep an eye on your social media presence. It especially monitors the social content and signals. Not only does your social media presence impact your rankings, but it's most likely that your social media profile will come up in the first page of your Google ranking.

Successful brands have a healthy social media presence. Although the ranking criteria is always changing, social media presence links your brand as valuable, credible and trustworthy.

Social media marketing may help improve your search engine rankings

There's a good chance that you're already focused on improving your search engine optimisation. But did you know that search engines may be using your social media presence as a factor in their rankings? Successful brands tend to have a healthy social media presence, so a strong social media presence may act as a signal to search engines that your brand is valuable, credible and trustworthy. Though the ranking factors are always changing, it's a safe bet that active social media channels will end up helping you in the end.

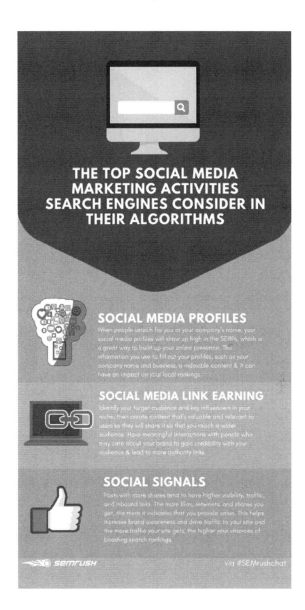

Your competitors are already on social media

Regardless of the industry annual target market, there is a good chance that your competition is already on the social media channels. This not only suggests that there is an opportunity for your brand, but it also suggests that your brand may already be talking to your competition on social media.

If you want to remain competitive on digital media, you will want to start building your presence. Social media content doesn't only show your brand personality, but it also communicates the latest message in a broadcast. On top of that, it shows your expertise and knowledge to potential leads. This is the best way you can set yourself apart from the competition.

Social media traffic leads to higher conversion rates

The most powerful area of social media convergence is bringing the human element to a brand. Since social media is a meeting place for consumers to socialise, brands are able to show their human side in a conversation, which in turns shows the company their personality.

Social media helps improve brand loyalty

This is a key tool for small businesses since they can't compete against the bigger companies that have bigger loyalty programmes. Social media is an effective way to build relationships with customers, which leads to greater loyalty and brand satisfaction over time. Various studies have shown that brands that engage with their clients and target audiences over social media, get repeat business from their customers.

The stronger the relationship that you build up with your customers on social media, the more it will set you apart from your competition. By engaging your clients with valuable and insightful content, and having a conversation about that content, you can turn your happy customers into your brand ambassadors.

Word of mouth marketing

Word of mouth goes a long way in marketing your brand. It's free, and it goes a long way in building trust. Social media has become a way for people to share their recommendations. By sharing the products, or having a conversation with their friends and family, it effectively becomes the new outlet of word of mouth. As a brand, you should be encouraging your customers to leave reviews and testimonials.

With customers likely buying from brands that have been recommended to them, you are in turn turning their friends and family into many influencers to buy your products.

Q7. **Because of social media, I am more likely to:**

80%	Try new things based on friends' suggestions
74%	Encourage my friends to try new products
72%	Stay more engaged with the brands I like
42%	Share any negative experiences with brands or products
32%	Not buy certain products because I learned of a negative customer experience

72% OF CONSUMERS TRUST ONLINE REVIEWS AS MUCH AS PERSONAL RECOMMENDATIONS FROM REAL PEOPLE *SEARCH ENGINE LAND*

68% OF CONSUMERS GO TO SOCIAL NETWORKING SITES TO READ PRODUCT REVIEWS *VOCUS*

90% OF CONSUMERS SAY THAT POSITIVE ONLINE REVIEWS INFLUENCE THEIR BUYING DECISIONS *DIMENSIONAL RESEARCH*

Not only do consumers trust reviews on social media, but they often seek them out before making a purchasing decision.

In the statistics, you will notice that it will suggest that consumers use social media to verify and review a brand. Hence, it is important that your happy customers leave a review about your products and services. This is a great way to encourage organic traffic for your funnels.

Find the new customers that you never knew existed

There are fundamentally two ways to acquire customers: proactively and reactively. Customers coming to your website via PPC or search engines, are customers that you are pulling reactively. This means that unless you proactively pull customers, you are missing out on a large chunk of your market.

One market opportunity that social media offers is through social listening. By following hashtags, you can see who is taking part in a conversation. This in turn gives your business the opportunity to look into who's buying your service, and an opportunity to understand which influences you may be able to partner with to boost your brand visibility.

Improve your brand presence

The more social media users use your content, the more people will talk about your brand. The more conversation that happens around your brand, the more coverage you will get in social media. Social media is always trying to promote the most talked about topics; hence, the more conversation there is, the better it is for your brand coverage. This is especially true when others share your content with their fans and followers.

This is a very important part of positioning your brand as a leader in the marketplace. So, the more people share, the more conversation they have, and the more comments they make, the more brand presence you will get.

Find out what your customers are thinking about

This is crucial for billing around. In social media, people talk, and if you follow what your audience is talking about, you will get valuable insights into what they're talking about. You can find out what they care about the most and, in return, you can develop your content around these concerns. Basically, by tapping into social media, you are able to find what your customers are interested in and what is driving them.

Because of the huge amount of data that social media carries on individuals, you are able to see your clients' behaviours and interests. This in turn means that you can look across all the posts and interactions across channels to figure out what works and what doesn't.

There are various analytics tools available within social media platforms and from third parties, which tell you what your clients do in general, which in turn means that the content that you develop will address their interests and behaviours.

Notes

Notes

Notes

References

1600 – Galileo Galilei discovers the principle of inertia, building the stage for a rational view of motion.

1600 – William Gilbert finds that Earth has magnetic poles and acts like a huge magnet.

1600 – Galileo Galilei discovers that projectiles move with a parabolic trajectory.

1608 – Hans Lippershey invents the refracting telescope, which Galileo soon puts to use.

1609 – Galileo Galilei observes moons of Jupiter, disproving church dogma that all movement in the universe is centred on Earth.

1609 – Johannes Kepler publishes his first two laws of planetary motion showing that planets move in elliptical orbits around the sun.

1610 – John Napier publishes tables of logarithms, showing how they can be used to accelerate calculations.

1619 – Kepler publishes his third law of planetary motion relating the time taken for a planet to orbit the sun with its distance from the sun.

1621 – Willebrord Snell discovers the laws of light refraction.

1628 – Kepler publishes his planetary tables, the calculations for which would have taken years without Napier's logarithms.

1629 – Nicolaus Cabeus finds there are two types of electric charge and notes both attractive and repulsive forces acting.

1632 – William Oughtred invents the slide rule. With the combined power of logarithms and slide rules, calculation speeds explode.

1632 – Galileo Galilei finds that the laws of motion are the same in all inertial reference frames.

1637 – René Descartes invents the Cartesian coordinate system – i.e. the x–y axis for graphs, allowing changes in quantities with time to be plotted.

1645 – Blaise Pascal invents the adding machine.

1652 – Thomas Bartholin discovers the human lymphatic system.

1662 – Robert Boyle publishes his law of pressure and volume in gases.

1654 – Blaise Pascal and Pierre de Fermat invent the mathematics of probability and statistics.

1656 – Christiaan Huygens discovers Saturn's rings after building a new telescope – the world's best.

1657 – Pierre de Fermat uses the principle of least time in optics.

1658 – Jan Swammerdam discovers the red blood cell.

1660 – Otto von Guerkicke builds a rotating sphere from which sparks fly. Static electricity can now be generated. He demonstrates electrostatic repulsion.

1660 – Robert Hooke discovers that the extension of a spring or elastic material is directly proportional to the applied force.

1661 – Robert Boyle writes The Sceptical Chymist, with his manifesto for the science of chemistry, explaining the roles of elements and compounds, and telling scientists they must carefully observe, record and report scientific data.

1633 – James Gregory publishes his design for the world's first reflecting telescope.

1664 – Robert Hooke uses a microscope to observe the cellular basis of life.

1665 – Isaac Newton invents calculus – the mathematics of change – without which we could not understand the modern world. He keeps it secret, using it to develop theories, which he eventually publishes in 1687.

1666 – Isaac Newton discovers that light is made up of all of the colours of the rainbow, which are refracted by different amounts in a glass prism.

1667 – Isaac Newton builds the world's first reflecting telescope.

1668 – John Wallis discovers the principle of conservation of momentum, one of the foundations of modern physics.

1669 – Hennig Brand becomes the first identifiable person to have discovered and isolated a new chemical element, phosphorus.

1674 – Antony van Leeuwenhoek discovers microorganisms.

1675 – Robert Boyle shows that electric repulsion and attraction act in a vacuum.

1676 – Ole Christensen Roemer measures the speed of light for the first time.

1676 – Christiann Huygens finds light can be refracted and diffracted and should be considered to be a wave-like phenomenon.

1684 – Gottfried Leibniz publishes his calculus, which he discovered independently of Isaac Newton. He has been working on calculus for the past decade.

1687 – Isaac Newton publishes one of the most important scientific books ever: Philosophiae Naturalis Principia Mathematica, revolutionizing physics and our understanding of gravity and motion. This was a momentous century in which science moved from a state of knowledge that was in many ways little more advanced than third century BC Greece to a much more advanced, sophisticated position, paving the way for the Industrial Revolution in the 1700s, and many more famous scientists. Probably the greatest advantage that Renaissance scientists had over their Ancient Greek predecessors was: The invention of the movable type printing press in 1450 by Johannes Gutenberg. (Bi Sheng invented movable type printing much earlier, in about 1040 AD in China, but this does not appear to have influenced the Renaissance.)

Leonardo Fibonacci brought the Hindu-Arabic number system to Europe in 1202 AD. The Greek number system was primitive, making calculations cumbersome, and confining most Greek mathematical achievements to geometry. European scientists were using the Roman system, which was not much better. The familiar Hindu-Arabic system of 0, 1, 2, 3, 4, 5, 6, 7, 8, 9... brought with it ease of calculation and the recognition that zero was a number in its own right. Mathematical rules for the correct use of zero were first written in 628 AD in

Brahmagupta's book *Brahmasputha Siddhanta*. This book also highlighted the use of negative numbers in, for example, solutions of quadratic equations. Following the huge scientific advances of the 1600s, we have continued to take enormous strides in scientific knowledge, carrying us to where we are today.

More importantly, I thank Mr. Raymond Aaron, *New York Times* top 10 best-selling author, and my personal mentor and coach, and his team for assisting me with my book.

There are many more people I could thank, but time, space, and modesty compel me to stop here.

About the Author

Sam Mahmud is a serial entrepreneur, technologist and an award-winning author. Sam has been at the forefront of digital marketing and has been instrumental in making many of the brands profitable.

This award-winning author started his career in an international organisation, and his career spans across investment banks in London, and hedge funds in Wall Street, New York. The author currently lives in London and runs his own advertising agency.

The author is a highly sought-after business coach, consultant and marketer, and he constantly develops cutting-edge tactics to help businesses all around the world. His passion is to build integrated, scalable, future-proof and ROI-focused digital marketing strategies to transform businesses online. He is one of those rare individuals who transitioned from a 9-to-5 job, to building several business portfolios of his own.

With this book, he shares his years of experience and in-depth blueprints that have helped many businesses and individuals across the world to increase their bottom line profits and decrease their overall costs.

Sam can be contacted directly via
sam@onepagegameplan.com.

Tools and resources mentioned in this book are available at
www.onepagegameplan.com.

Printed in Great Britain
by Amazon

74845739R00069